P is for PAUL the Apostle

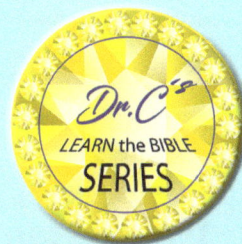

Dr. C. White-Elliott

Illustrated by Sidra Mehmood

CLF

www.clfpublishing.org
909.315.3161

Cover design by Senir Design. Contact info: info@senirdesign.com

Illustrations by Sidra Mehmood of Fivver.com

ISBN #978-1-945102-72-1

Printed in the United States of America.

Dedicated to all who may have

misunderstood the gospel of Jesus Christ

but have received revelation knowledge.

Once upon a time, in a land far, far away was a very powerful man. Many people looked up to him, showing much respect. But, there were many other people who were scared of him because many times he could be very mean. The man's name was Saul, and he was born in a city called Tarsus.

When Saul was a teenager, he studied under a man who taught him a lot about Jewish laws and customs. Saul's teacher's name was Gamaliel. After studying for several years, Saul took all he learned and made it a big part of his life. He lived by all the laws and customs he learned, and he wanted others to do the same.

After Jesus died on the cross, He left behind many people who followed His teachings. However, Saul did not agree with Jesus' teachings. He thought they went against the Word of God. But, Jesus is God's son, and He was teaching everything His father told Him to teach. Because Saul did not know the truth, he went from town to town throwing people who followed Jesus' teaching in jail or causing them harm.

One day, Saul decided to travel to another city to harm more of Jesus' followers. To his surprise, a bright light shined down from heaven, and a voice said, "Saul, Saul, why do you persecute me?" It was the voice of Jesus that was calling to Saul. As he heard the voice, Saul was knocked to the ground.

When Saul finally stood up, he could not see anything. All around him was darkness. Finally, Saul realized he was blind, and he stayed blind for three days. Speaking again from heaven, Jesus told Saul to go to a house and to stay there for a while. Jesus had a plan for Saul's life.

When Saul could see again, God had changed his name to Paul and had changed his heart. Paul no longer wanted to hurt people who loved Jesus. Instead, he wanted to tell everyone he could about Jesus, so they could get to know and love him, too. Paul went from city to city telling people about Jesus, hoping they would make Jesus their Lord and Savior.

Eventually, Paul became an apostle for God. An apostle is a person who tells other people about God as they go from one city to the next. Also, they establish churches, so people will have a place to worship together. Paul, along with other apostles, began to start churches in many cities, so the gospel of Jesus Christ could be preached and heard.

Day by day, people joined the church and gave their life to Jesus. Paul was very happy. But, many people were upset about Paul talking about Jesus, just as he once had been. To try and stop him, he was arrested and thrown in jail.

Paul loved God the Father and Jesus, God the Son, so much that he did not allow the fact that he was in jail to stop him from telling people about the love of God. He began to write letters to the different churches to encourage them to keep sharing God's Word with other people.

From that point forward, Paul was in and out of jail, between his travels from one city to another. Many times, Apostle Paul traveled by boat or ship, and he usually had someone along with him. Through all the good times and bad, Paul had joy in his heart because he was spreading the Good News of Jesus. He did the work of a faithful servant because he loved God with all his heart. He did not allow anyone to stop him from what he believed to be the right thing to do.

There is a lot we can learn from Apostle Paul's life. One of the main things is no matter what beliefs you have in life, always be willing to be open for new information to be shared with you. Like Paul, the ideas you have could be false. Listening to someone else share a different view could change your life just as it did for Paul the Apostle.

www.ingramcontent.com/pod-product-compliance
Lightning Source LLC
Chambersburg PA
CBHW041957100426
42813CB00019B/2917